I0407193

INSIDE DA G!

A Guide, Manual & Explanation

Trevor Flip Robinson

Edited by Mike Valentino

Organized by Marie Delus

funhouse ent

twitter.com/Queenzflip

Inside Da G.

Copyright © 2009 by Trevor - flip - Robinson

ISBN # 9781466362512

Printed in USA

DEDICATION

A Special Note To All My Supporters

I have done a lot of things in my life that I'm not proud of, but it's my Supporters and my family that keep me afloat and give me the determination to write this book.

I especially want to acknowledge my Mom, Marie Delus, for arranging some of my thoughts and adding an idea here and there.

This is from my heart; it doesn't get any realer than this. Please read and respect my views on life and relationships, because it's not every day you see 22 year olds writing books about relationships.

I appreciate you and love you all.

Thank You

CONTENTS

SPECIAL ACKNOWLEDGEMENTS

PREFACE

I just got up one day and decided to write this book. Some of these subjects apply to me and things I've witnessed or experienced. I researched and obtained quotes and definitions from other sources; such as: www.wikihow.com*; but this book is completely my personal opinion on life.

Trevor QueenzFlip Robinson is a Rapper who got in the Game young, and experienced more in a few short years than most do in a lifetime. This book offers his no-holds-barred opinions on what makes a relationship work, why they don't work, and how you can fix them. It's also a guide to pinpoint specific issues that people from all walks of life have to cope with every day in our hectic and often crazy world. Trevor offers down to earth, no-nonsense advice showing you how to overcome all of the stress that comes your way when life starts taking its toll on you. Hey, here's the good news: there are solutions. There are answers. Now you just have to read the book…. **Mike Valentino**

NOTE (DISCLAIMER): THIS IS A SHORT BOOK, THE CHAPTERS ARE IN RANDOM ORDER; SOME OF THE CHAPTERS DON'T COINICIDE SO BARE WITH ME AND ENJOY.

INTRODUCTION

My name is Trevor Flip Robinson. I am 22, I am not an expert on relationships but I've been through a lot and have seen a lot in my days of living. A lot of us look for love in the wrong places. There is nothing wrong with that, we are all human, but I am here to teach you, how to spot and differentiate the G (GAME) before you get into it. And if you're currently in it, how to save yourself from years of heartache and pain.

Marie Delus foreword: Flip's introduced his project by handing me a draft document to read. Upon reading the piece, my immediate emotion was "embarrassment" and as I continued to read, I experienced a lot of TMI moments. However, I understood the piece and knowing my son, realized his words and insight will have an impact. The piece motivated me to join him in completing his book. My initial plan was to help him edit the book, as I read his stories I became motivated to not only rearrange his topics but introduce other subject-matters that I felt were also important. I believe his personal experiences and honesty will communicate to the youths of today. I hope you enjoy the book as much as I had helping complete it.

CHAPTER ONE

WHAT IS LOVE

I've heard or read once that "Love is many splendid things"; Nahhhhhhh…

What is the definition of love? The dictionary definition is:

A person toward whom love is felt; beloved person.

1.   A profoundly tender, passionate affection for another person.

2.   A feeling of warm personal attachment or deep affection, as for a parent, child, or friend.

3.   Sexual passion or desire.

My definitions are:

1.   BLINDED BY UNCONTROLABLE AFFECTION TOWARDS YOUR PARTNER.

2.   LOVE IS A TRAIT THAT PEOPLE TEND TO FOLLOW JUST BECAUSE OTHERS ARE GOOD AT IT.
3.   A FEELING IN OUR BODIES THAT MAKE US DO THE MOST UNIMAGINABLE THINGS THAT WILL HAVE OUR, GREAT, GREAT, GREAT, GRANDPARENTS ROLLING IN THEIR GRAVES.

Now don't get me wrong, back in the day people used to meet in train stations, get a case of "love at first sight," marry within three days, and remain married for 20+ years. But that was back then, when men and women took the relationship theory more seriously; nowadays people look at relationships as a competition with one another, by trying to see who can hurt who more or cause the most damage.

For example: Tom and Tina have been together for five years, they met at a bar and had instant chemistry. On that same night Tom and Tina booked a hotel room and knocked boots all-night long. From there they both cut each other partners off, in order to pursue their relationship. After six months, Tom and Tina started having numerous fights; after one year they had a child together. Two years later Tina caught Tom cheating and from there vowed revenge. Tina got Tom back by sleeping with one of his friends; but Tom forgave

her since Tina was bringing in all the money, and tried to work it out. Now by using your imagination where do you see their relationship heading?
I see two Nah!!!!!!! with this relationship:

They met in the club and had sex the same night; that's a no no. There's nothing wrong with a one night stand, I had numerous in my day, BUT let a one night stand remain a One night stand. No ifs, ands or buts about it, don't expect anything out of this transaction because your first impression of each other is based on sex. If you pursue a relationship and try to make it work then what do you really know about each other? I feel before you can commit to a relationship, you have to really get to know your partner, know their likes, dislikes; family if they have any and really become a friend more than anything.

1. I feel people who remain in relationships for a long time are close friends. They can tell when their partner is sick or having a bad day, and some people have a spiritual connection with one another. Now for those who don't believe in GOD or spirits don't be alarmed, because here's what I mean by spiritual connection. For example: a man can be at work and his wife is at home and let's say that the man gets sick; the wife will start to have a funny feeling in the pit of her stomach and she will know that something's wrong.

So if you're not going to take the time to really get to know someone, you should not try to pursue a relationship point blank.

Now as far as the example I gave you earlier about Tom and Tina, they should not have been in a relationship because they really did not get to know each other. It's like you're walking down the street, and a stranger opens their coat with nothing underneath and says screw me. **(Take a minute to think about what your reaction would be)**..................... I bet you didn't need that minute huh, you just said to yourself HELLLLLLLLLLLL NO, I DON'T KNOW WHAT THAT MOTHER FUCKER GOT.

Well, Tom and Tina are the same scenario but a different environment, classier, well not really classy but more upscale than the street. With Tom and Tina's situation they met in the club, Tom approached Tina, they both were probably intoxicated, music's loud so they possibly couldn't conduct a conversation, they exchanged phone numbers, and when the party was over then went to a hotel.

2. **Cutting off each other's partners,** without knowing if it's the right thing to jump into, is stupid. Always leave yourself enough room to weigh your options. ALWAYS!!!!!! Because by doing that, you will know who is who and what is what. If everything goes according to plan you can do what I

call **APROXIMATION OF ELIMINATION**. So that's a Nah to cutting off your partner right away. Remember you are entitled to talk to as many people as you want to, that's part of getting to know someone, but as long as you don't have sex with them, there's nothing wrong with making and having friends.

Now there's two Yesssirs.

If you decide on the one night stand:

1.   You should book a hotel, because you never know who is who, and they can rob you blind.

2.   Do it because you want to bust a Nut or have an orgasm not to get into a relationship.

Now if you got this far in my book, then that means you want to see where it goes from here. I'm going to warn you it gets worse, more belligerent and exposing the stupidity in people, blinded by what they think LOVE is. If you don't want to continue reading put my book down, throw it away for all I care. Obviously you're having a relationship issues or you wouldn't have this book in the first place; either you can't find the right man or woman, which is why you're reading this, so sit back, relax and learn.

ONE NIGHT STAND

Not everyone feels the need to have an emotional connection with someone in order to enjoy having sex. Yes, there are risks, but for some people the enjoyment outweighs those risks. Abstinence is the only way to avoid several issues (e.g. diseases) and most can be avoided or lessened with some forethought (e.g. condom). The other is YOUR personal opinion.

Not everyone looks at this subject the same way. Some people have one night stands because they have sex and love all mixed up in their heads, so they have sex in order to be loved. Of course it doesn't work, so they go out again and have sex again, and it's a vicious cycle. Other people just like sex, and they're not in the right frame of mind for a relationship. That's fine as long as they're sleeping with other single people. To be honest, I don't see the problem with casual sex in situations where nobody is in a monogamous relationship; so long as everyone is a consenting adult and uses a condom. It's only when the sex is irresponsible or done for the wrong reasons that it's a problem. Remember that nobody is forcing you to have casual sex or get involved with people that do.

We don't all have the same view of sex. Personally, I wouldn't have casual sex because it's not something that appeals to me. But if someone can do it, and enjoy it without compromising their own safety, it's not my place- or yours- to judge them. For not everyone who has one night stands, does it with a lot of people, fails to use protection, or does it when they're already in a relationship. So, what's wrong with having a bit of fun as long as you're safe? Some people can separate love from sex, especially men. As long as you both know where you stand, I don't see a problem with it. Love and sex are two different things. Sex is good, doesn't matter who it's with.

You believe it's not right, that's fair enough and you are entitled to your opinion, but you should also respect others. Maybe people don't want a relationship. A relationship is a huge commitment that includes lots of time and emotions, which in most cases leads to heartbreak. Some people just want the fun part without the hassles, and there is nothing wrong with that. If you are responsible, then there won't be any unwanted pregnancies or diseases. By the way, even married couples have unwanted pregnancies and can still give each other diseases.

PERSONAL EXPERIENCE

I met a girl in the club, and we kicked it off. I bought her drinks, etc. etc. etc. Now at this time of my life I was seventeen; I used to hang with the older people cause my cousin was in the industry. He used to let me hold down his Dodge Magnum when it first came out; so you can imagine how I acted. It was on 24/7. Anyway, so I'm stuntin, bring her back to the crib, she put it on me, we went to sleep then I wake up and all my money is gone, my ring and mad other shit. How? What did I do wrong? Well, I should have booked a hotel. LOL – Lesson Learned.

CHAPTER TWO

GAME

At my age I've seen a lot of people who play love like a game.

The dictionary definition: Competitive activity involving skill, chance, or endurance on the part of two or more persons who play according to a set of rules, usually for their own amusement or for that of spectators.

2nd definition: A trick or strategy.

My definition of game: a facade that's portrayed, by oneself in order to get a goal accomplished whether it's for money, sex, etc.

We as human beings have to learn how to read through a game. Sometimes we know it's a game but choose to ignore it. Why? If you know deep down in your heart or in the back of your mind someone is running game, a.k.a. G., then why don't you stop them in their tracks? Are you so desperate that you prefer to be subjected to the nonsense and go through the heartache and pain? Yes, you are.

First things first, I want you to say this to yourself:

I AM NOT WEAK MINDED AND I WILL NOT LET A GAME OVERSHADOW MY BELIEFS.

Now say it aloud. I don't care where you're at, train, bus, school, home, say it aloud.

I AM NOT WEAK MINDED AND I WILL NOT LET A GAME OVERSHADOW MY BELIEFS.

Now what do I mean by overshadow your beliefs? I mean, you know and sense the bullshit, you know he/she is lying, but you choose to ignore it because you want to go through the same shit over and over and over and over again.

GAME A.K.A. G SCENARIOS
HERE ARE A NUMBER OF FACTORS IN THE GAME A.K.A. G SCANERIOS.

COMPETITION AMONG FRIENDS FOR PRIDE OR RANKS AMONGST FRIENDS: A lot of us; well, I am 22, so in my circles we used to compete to get girls. Who can hit it first, who can get the number, sometimes we will see if we can smash the same girl. AIN'T THAT A BITCH. This happens all over the world, people play what I call the "who can fuck her first," or "I will fuck her before you" game. Just for RANKS. Is it right? No, but who are we to say what's right or what's wrong. In a situation like that both parties are to blame. Since some girls/women know that's your friend, knowing that she sexed you up and still end up fucking your friend or vice versa.

(Now don't think I am bashing women, men are as much to blame; but since I am a male and all my experience has been with the female species, I am going to use women's flaws as my reference first, then males.)

JUST WASN'T HONEST IN THE BEGINNING ABOUT HIS/HERS FEELINGS AND THE OUTCOME WHEN YOU DONT SHOW ATTENTION:

Why do people talk to you, commit sexual acts with you, then end up fucking your sister, brother, friend, cousin, mother, father, etc? Now don't get me wrong, you are entitled to your feelings and doing what you want to do, but from the gate you should let your feelings be known. If you want to fuck, then you want to fuck! But if you plan on taking it to the next level then act like it and don't send mixed signals.

Now I am about to let you know the rules of the game and how to prevent from getting caught up in that nonsense. First, my opinion is this: people who fuck your friends/family member are either trying to do two things:

a. Get back at you;

b. They always wanted to fuck this person and you were the first one they met.

In order to prevent getting involved with a situation like this, there are a few things you should know AND BE AWARE OF. First, if your friend **IS SINGLE** and wants to hook you up with someone, six times out of ten they had a crush on this person prior, or had sexual relations. Because if they believe this person is so great then it's a good chance they've kicked it first. So, always ask these questions: How did you meet this person? Aren't you single, so why wouldn't you want him/her for yourself? Well I have a few of answers for you:

a.   They either had sexual relations before and they got something over one another's head.

b. They had a mutual agreement and an understanding after they had sexual relations.

c. They liked each other and it just didn't work out.

Pay attention because when you and that person they hooked you up with kick it off, they will wonder why didn't they kick it off like that; ONE SIMPLE CONVERSATION **CAN CHANGE IT ALL.**

Once again this doesn't happen to everyone but this is for the person who has that gut feeling about their significant other.

Scenario:

Sherry: I see you and Tia really like each other.

John: Yeah, she's mad cool.

Sherry: I don't know where we went wrong, why we didn't kick it.

John: because you were a big **FRONTER (now he just threw the bait).**

Sherry: I never fronted on you.

You can imagine the rest, but this is just an example, of how one single convo can open up doors, or past portals into a messed up situation.

Ask questions in the beginning, make sure you investigate, and question everything. You do not want to be stuck between a rock and a hard place.

THAT EXCUSE HOLDS NO WATER.

Above are two game scenarios but some people say, it just happens, it just happened, shuuuuuuuuuuuut upppppp, with that "it just happened" excuse. It's like water off a duck's back; shit will never stick, GET IT!

Unless having sex with someone is your professional job, (then that's ok) other than that, **that "it just happened" excuse is NOT valid.**

We all know when our (significant other) introduces us to a good looking friend/family member, we say to ourselves wow, she looks good, or vice versa. We even go as far as to say, in a joking manner to our (significant other) like "yo such and such is real pretty" and what's the response 99% of us get? Oh you wanna fuck my friend/family member (lol).

In my opinion, your significant other and your friend/family member should not be that cool. I mean "hi" and "byes" are good, even a lil laugh here or there, cool; but phone conversation **NO**, meeting up with each other, for a get together, **NO**.

There should be no reason for these interactions to occur. Why? Ask yourself that question: Why should there be convo on the phone, a meet up, etc? What is so fucking important that you have to call my girl privately that I can't hear? Are you throwing me a surprise party? Well guess what my birthday is JULY 29 and we are in January. This is just an example; but what's the reason?

There should be **NO** reason that your man/woman should talk to your friend/family privately **AT ALL**. You might disagree with me, but this is just my opinion. Matter of fact, I take that back. Some family members and friends have a wonderful relationship, but that's only if the core of your relationship is solid, that only if in your heart you know this person is there for you all the way, then by all means.

Now you might say to yourself, well isn't that a sign of insecurity? Then I will answer your question with a question: Isn't it weird that you and your girl just had an argument, now she's at the movies or the bowling alley with your best friend or brother? Now when they finally confess that they've been secretly seeing each other, you are so shocked and shocked. I will break down for you in lamest terms the steps, what you should look out for to know whether your significant other and family member are interested in each other.

Wait! Before I continue, I wanna let the readers know that there are a lot of friends/family members that's very cool and wouldn't even think of looking at one another in that way. Also, some people are so friendly that the other party might get the wrong signal. It's not intentional; it's just that they want a lot of attention. However, if in your heart you feel that your girl/man is extra flirtatious or your friend/family member is, then read my steps and follow the next chapter.

CHAPTER THREE

FAMILY/FRIENDS & SIGNIFICANT OTHER DO'S AND DON'T'S

There are do's and don't when it comes to family/friends relationship towards your significant others. I think family/friends:

•   Should not talk to your significant other on the phone, after hours. Deadline should be 9 p.m., earlier if possible.

•   Should not be extra touchy feely with your significant other, a pat on the back is ok, a handshake, but an unnecessary hug during an outburst   of   laughter,   that's   a Nahhhhhhhhhhhhhhhh.

•   During a party they should not be off to the side talking, or in the kitchen or basement by themselves talking. I feel that there is nothing that you can tell my woman, that you can't tell me, and if it's a surprise party, call my mother and she'll relay the message.

Those are just examples. Once again these are my opinions and based on personal experiences; so take it or not.

The "get back at you" factor: This is simple, if you make your significant other mad, or MAD enough, they will fuck someone just to get back at you. This is scientifically proven, is it not? Well I say it is and it depends on who you ask. It depends on how mad you made them, and if you cheated. Ignore them to show a long time friend more attention; nine times out of ten they will cheat. When you compare them to your friend and make it seem like your friend is better that leads to jealousy. They will then want to show you that someone else will appreciate them.

NOW YOU MAY ASK THE #1 QUESTION THAT MILLIONS OF POPLE ASK. WHY DO PEOPLE CHEAT?

My personal opinion is that people cheat for their own selfish reasons. Basically, wanting their cake and eating it too. But believe it or not sometimes it's hard to tell someone it's over; especially, if you have a conscience. Or you just don't wanna let go like that; it may be the sex or that this person is the sole provider. It may be for numerous reasons; look at it like this, if you have a job paying $17 an hour, and someone told you about a job that's paying $22 an hour, would you quit your job without knowing you have the other job in the bag? Same thing with people who like to cheat on their significant other, they can't just leave you alone without knowing what they're getting into, if it's concrete, or if the outcome will be the same.

Now check this out, nine times out of ten, the person you cheat with will more than likely become your main. Now that they are your main, they will always have it in the back of their mind that you've cheated on your previous partner so they think it's OK to cheat on you. Or, in some situations, the number two position, will get bored with the wifey position, because now you're giving them your 100% attention and she (he) is the kind of person who loves to break up happy homes, so they will turn around and cheat on you. It's a cycle, and most likely that **CYCLE IS FULL WITH KARMA**. And you know what they say about karma and what a bitch she is…

The only way to stop the cycle is to be honest with the person you're dealing with by letting them know you wanna keep your options open. If they really care they will work harder to gain your attention and full time on them. Or **JUST DON'T CHEAT. YOU CAN DO IT.**

The "attention" factor: If you're ignoring your significant other, how long do you think they can take it? Honestly, how long can someone take the abuse? Why do I call it abuse? Cause it makes the person second guess the reason why they are with you. They blame themselves for your behavior, which in turn make them stressed, which causes them to be sick, etc. So that's a form of abuse.

Even the married woman whose mind is in a trance eventually meets that person who makes her feel good, regardless of the outcome. Regardless of how long they've been with you, someone else can still occupy their mind. When you see a drastic change, for example, when you come home and talk to your significant other but their whole demeanor is different, you should know something is up. Or are you so into yourself that you can't see they are straying away? You see, we human beings have a selfish way of basically not caring about the other person's feelings, but then when our significant other leaves us we are so APPALLED.

My suggestion is to take some time out your day and show the significant other some attention; send flowers; make a call, ask how you doing? The little things will keep you in good graces for a week, but big things like jewelry, will keep you good for a month, LOL, just joking. Seriously, take the time out and be attentive and you will see the difference.

The "alternative" Factor:

Now think about when you're in the limelight, at a party scene, going out every night and have a lot of friends. You most likely will not take your significant other's feelings into consideration, so he/she is bound to go find it somewhere else. My advice is if you're getting bored and shit, try to do something to spice it up. If that doesn't work, take time to yourself, but know when you take time to yourself, you tend to miss the person you have been around for so long.

Being around a person 24/7, 7 days a week 365 days a year can become annoying. Why you think people work to all hours of the night? They don't wanna come home and hear the nig nagging and those are the people that remain married for a long time. They decide on different outcomes. Some people who been involved for so long, they just don't want to get a divorce, cause they have so much invested into their relationship. We all wish we can have a Titanic kind of love but that's not how the world works. So some people should just have an understanding, **AN OPEN RELATIONSHIP.**

PERSONAL EXPERIENCE

Now this story is a bit different, I met this girl at the mall, it was like love at first sight. We exchanged numbers, and KICKED it off instantly. Our phone convo, and everything was perfect.

Now when I meet someone that passes the attractive mark, I become overzealous. I have a cousin, quiet, smoother than me about two years older; very popular. So she and I was kicking it and I brought her to the BLOCK, 118TH N MERRICK BLVD, lol, hell has no wrath compared to that block. So I brought her over there and I noticed that when I introduced her to my cousin she smiled longer than was necessary. I didn't think anything of it, that's my cousin; she knows better, matter of fact they both know better. So they laughing giggling, she was patting his back, well not patting but like one tap on the back. So at the end of the night we left, and I asked her the question in a joking manner; "YOU WANNA FUCK MY COUSIN?" She immediately got defensive, "No! He's mad cool, come on what do I look like." Granted, I let it go. About a week later, my cousin calls me and says he bumped into her on Jamaica Ave.

What he didn't tell me was that they exchanged numbers. So I'm chilling with her one day and see my cousin calling her phone; I answered. He laughed it off; I did also and we left it alone. So now about three months pass and she and I are going good; it was about 12:00 a.m. and I am driving on Merrick Blvd and guess who I see leaving my cousin's house? EXXXXACTLY; USE YOUR IMAGINATION FOR *THE REST.*

CHAPTER FOUR

FAÇADE

I'm going to move away from love and relationship to discuss what makes a "G"; not a "G" for game but a "G" for "Gamer"; sometimes known as a fake G. Most gamers have a façade; **there are three type of Façade:**

The Hook-up Façade:

Now we all fall into the façade stage once in a while. What do I mean by Hook-up façade? The way we pick and choose who to give a chance to, simply by the way they look or what they got. By, the way, I don't respect this type of façade; I mean we like who we like, but everyone deserves a fair chance.

Here's an example, a lot of girls say they wanna take it slow, and get to know you, right? Bear with me. They tell you they wanna get to know you, and take the slowest time in the world to make a move. Ok, that's fair I concur; but have you ever noticed, if a popular or good looking guy asks her out or even if she likes you, they will have sex within a week?

Seriously now, I know that's not all women, so don't get offended (so bear with me, ladies), but there's always that person who you'll give it up faster to than the other. Why though? Is it fair to the guy that put all the footwork in? This is where karma comes back in; when you leave the foot worker for the pretty boy, and shit doesn't work out, you become distraught. Take a minute and think about it…

Now do you get my drift? Think about the boy that really liked you, the boy that was always there and you went for the next man. Fellas aren't off the hook; they do the same thing.

Let me explain something to you females and males; both species like challenges. Our problem is we look for the challenges in the wrong places.

Let me explain:

Females, you, like the pretty boy, the guy all the girls like and the guy that pays you the least attention, right? But I bet you didn't know that when he stands you up, even though you want him more and more, he's not even thinking about you, that's why he stood you up.

A guy that's in the limelight, popular, etc, can invite six girls to his house at one time. Three out of those six, he would end up wanting to sex up, that is, if he can fit all three in his schedule. If not then, two or one can do. So Miss Lady, you're basically a lottery ticket. So while you're ignoring the guy who yearns for your attention, the guy whose attention you want ignores you.

With the above in mind; now let us talk about **Material Façade**:

A lot of people act like they have it all but really don't. A person who gets paid $500 a week, after taxes they will bring home about $1,500 a month. A fake G will go shopping for a party, spend their last dime on clothing but won't have money to buy a drink or take a cab home. Now people get mad when they find out that the person who portrayed this big façade is a fraud. Sometimes it's too late, you're already in it too deep. My best advice is to **investigate** and basically have your own shit, period. It is terrible how someone gets in the club, pulls out all their rent money, spends it, and then has the nerve to ask you for money for a cab. Stuff like that is ridiculous but we all basically get caught up in the hype and try to be something we're not. It's ok to be yourself!

I had a case of the **fraudulent flu:** acting like I was something I wasn't – perpetrating a façade; then reality struck, and I had to cut it out because I was put on blast. Everyone knows when you are put on blast and it's not a good thing ,especially when the evidence against you is substantial. **My advice to everyone again is to be you.**

The "Help that builds your façade": I mean when a person builds another from the ground up and that person turns from a zero to a hero.

For example, a woman who turns an unattractive guy into an attractive guy was basically tired of the bullshit and decided to go another route. She was tired of getting played, tired of the lies and deceit; so she gets an ugly guy and makes him into a good looking "G". Little did she know she was about to repeat it all over again. You can not build a guy up and expect his confidences not to peak. You thought he would cater to you? Well you thought wrong. The mere fact that you thought that makes you crazy; in my opinion. All you did was boosted his ego and made the other girl's job easy. When he was a zero no one looked his way, right? Now that he's a hero everyone wants to be saved. My suggestion is to not do it at all and if you do, make sure the ball is always in your court; meaning, show him that it doesn't bother you that he got all the girls wanting to be saved. Trust me it'll work. Cause remember, he never experienced this type of attention before, so try to be as understanding as you can, let him explore but make sure the ball remains in your court.

CHAPTER FIVE

INSECURITIES/LACK OF CONFIDENCE

Sine I talked about a "zero" in my last chapter; I want to take a moment to talk about what makes someone a "zero"; sometimes it's because of looks but. most of the time it's because of a lack of confidence.

Insecurities and nervousness are emotions that protect us some of the time. They can be described as little caution flags that come up as we face risky circumstances in life. If you ever felt insecure when a drunk friend asked for a key to drive you home, you probably benefited from that insecurity. Or maybe someone at a party made you feel nervous, so you left, later to find out that he had done something bad. Again, the feelings were helpful for you. In fact, a person who genuinely feels no insecurities or nervousness is probably very dangerous to be around. They are like carnival riders, who like the dangers of roller coasters; they play with emotions for the enjoyment of the rider.

Lack of confidence or assurance:

First things first, as a single male, lack of confidence can be a red flag for females. If you don't show confidence she will either look somewhere else or walk all over you. If you display this weakness she will capitalize on it, for example:

> Let's say you're a nice dresser but not such a good looker; however, since you have paper (money), you have confidence because of the substantial amount of attention you're getting. But to a certain extent, a pretty female will see you as a gold mine (not all pretty females; I'm talking about the ones who take advantage). Once she put IT on you, she'll have you singing, spending money; just because she filled that void in your life. There is nothing wrong with buying your shorty something, but if you're doing all the giving and not receiving, there's a problem. It's supposed to be a 50/50; if you're just spending then your friends will see/say that you are stupid.

> Now, ladies, you tend to go for the guy who appears to have the most confidence, handsome, etc., without knowing that in some or even in the majority of cases he has more insecurity than the average guy. To help with his insecurities, if you truly care, you would

try to understand and help him as a friend, let him know you're interested but that you're also there for him.

Believe it or not we all have a case of insecurity. The cockiest persons in the world have some form of insecurity; unless you are a sociopath (then you don't give a damn about anything).

Being insecure, having a lack of confidence, can also be dangerous to your health. For example, rich people get rid of their insecurities by getting plastic surgery; mostly to try to please people and be something they're not. Think about it, why would you change your look? Why would you get fresh, fly, etc? For your own satisfaction? If so then that's fine and dandy; if not you're an IDIOT. Confidence is one of the main keys to a healthy and strong relationship, PERIOD. If you show a lack of confidence then you're headed into a brick wall.

A couple of examples of insecurities:

Persistence Nervousness: The feelings of insecurity and nervousness are there almost all the time regardless of the situation; it usually means you have a bad worry habit or a mild anxiety problem. Severe anxieties can be very limiting, so, if you suspect you have severe anxiety then get help. It's normal to blow it (mess up) under stressful situations from time to time. It isn't normal to blow it (mess up) all the time...this is performance-limiting nervousness. People get this in situations from public speaking to sports, and from dating to doctor visits. If you blow it (mess up) regularly because of nervousness or insecurities, you should address the problem; especially if it is limiting your relationships or job performance.

Limited Participation: If nervousness or insecurities cause you to occasionally choose not to participate in an activity or take a job then these fears are limiting your life. If it regularly prevents you from participating in normal activities, it's likely we're talking about performance and social anxieties.

What Are Some Causes of Nervousness and Insecurities...Does Low Self-Esteem Play a Role? A serious loss or tragedy from the past can change how some people see everything. This is usually the root of a serious anxiety disorder rather than nervousness or insecurities. I had a friend who lost a leg in an auto accident and from then on was very agitated every time she got in a car...this is an anxiety...not just insecurity.

Low self-esteem is usually the chief cause of nervousness and insecurity problems. It's rooted in the feelings of fear about "measuring up" or doing something embarrassing. The bad news is...you won't measure up to your standard of perfection and you will do embarrassing things. The good news is...everyone is in the same boat. This is very good news...read it again. This means that there is nothing unusual about a little fuck up every now and then. So try to relax! A lot of you are reading this and saying he's crazy -- well then put THE BOOK DOWN.

CHAPTER SIX

SELF-ESTEEM.

Insecurities and nervousness can limit your life and relationship. Most of the time it takes self-esteem to help you overcome these feelings.

Definition of self-esteem: A realistic respect for or favorable impression of oneself; self-respect.

Self-esteem plays a major role in finding someone and having a relationship. In relationships a lack of self-esteem would put you in a lot of bad situations. Having high self-esteem brings the best out of relationships; it makes your significant other feel proud to be yours, and in turn try their best to make you happy. It's basically having respect for your self, knowing you can accomplish anything. By having high self-esteem and confidence it also lets your significant other know that you can hold down the fort if necessary.

On the opposite side, low self-esteem leads to a lot of negative things. First off, when your self-esteem is low, you become sluggish, you think everyone is better than you. Now how the fuck are you going to keep a woman/man if you do not have faith in yourself? You have to fix yourself before you can make a commitment.

WHAT CAUSES LOW SELF-ESTEEM?

Personal issues in a person's life can cause low self-esteem. It may be that they have been knocked back in a job or they have a bad split up in a relationship. Low self-esteem is difficult to get out of, but thinking and acting positively should be a start to having a positive effect on your self-esteem.

Sometimes I have low self-esteem?

Low self-esteem can be caused by many, many factors: getting teased when you are a kid; always being told you can't do anything right; having a health problem that makes you feel inferior to others; getting rejected when you ask someone out; not being happy with your body; and many more facts of life.

A SCENARIO of a Girl with low Self-esteem:

Lately I have been feeling fat and ugly. I feel like none of my clothes fit me and everyone around me is skinny. I'm pretty sure I'm not fat and I try to tell myself I'm not but I can't help feeling that way. I also feel like I'm fucked up, especially around pretty girls. Other times I feel good about myself and my body. I feel like I'm two people and I don't have a healthy image of myself.

Controlling and Overcoming Insecurities and Nervousness:

Remember insecurities and nervousness from the previous chapter and the roller coaster...how we tricked our mind into thinking we were in danger? Nervousness and insecurities are like our minds tricking us into thinking there is danger when there isn't. Like the roller coaster, we make our thoughts do the opposite; get control over our insecurities. Instead of thinking 'what if?' we learn to think 'so what!' For example, most performers (speakers, singers, etc.) feel their performance isn't up to par, but being nervous beforehand can give them a dramatic edge; even their mistakes are entertaining. No one sees your mistakes like you do.

I remember feeling particularly insecure for a few months and finally asked my mom if she was disappointed in me or felt I was a failure. She said she was impressed by me, and then listed a half dozen of my accomplishments that she felt were amazing. I still have insecurities and nervousness, but now I know it's just my mind taking me on a roller-coaster ride.

If this isn't enough, then pull your calendar out and build a task list. List all of life's normal things that make you feel nervous or insecure...and do them! Yes, do them! Prove to yourself that the world will not come to an end. Do them regularly and repeatedly. The bigger the insecurity, the more you have to confront it. You won't believe how powerful you'll feel when you do all the things that you were scared to do in the past. This will build your self-esteem like nothing else. Sometimes our nervousness and insecurities are so big we need extra help; if so then ask for help from family, friends or God to break the fear.

EXAMPLES OF HOW DO YOU OVERCOME LOW SELF-ESTEEM

You should sit down and think about you and not let other people decide what it is that makes you feel good. For example, you can spend more time getting ready on the weekends to make yourself feel pretty. Maybe having your hair done a certain way or how certain clothes fit on you. Once you know what it is that makes you feel your very best, try to achieve at least one of these things that makes you feel beautiful every day. Then you have no reason to ever feel ugly and fat because you have made sure that you are comfortable and happy with yourself before you leave the house.

On a side note, those who bully may have low self-esteem because they aren't happy unless someone else is not.

Remember, everyone has they own issues, I am not here to judge; no one can judge us but GOD, but we all as humans have to try and control our emotions and try our best to help others overcome their insecurities and low self-esteem.

<u>Overcoming Low Self-Esteem Phase:</u>

Overcoming a low self-esteem is never easy. However, just as anything else in life one must do all that can be done to change this feeling. Many times you may hear, "people can only do to you what you allow them to." Well, that statement is partially true, because you can control of yourself; you can keep from feeling bad about yourself no matter what others say. However, if you were exposed to verbal, physical, mental and/or emotional abuse, it is harder to change the perception of yourself. In that case, surround yourself with positive people. Here are more methods to overcome a low self-esteem:

<u>RID ALL THE NEGATIVE PEOPLE IN YOUR LIFE!!!</u>

DOES NOT show a huge amount of gratitude when someone compliments you, although it is a nice gesture, you deserve it, so saying "thank you" is enough. Also, DO NOT "fish" for more compliments, it looks desperate.

Treat yourself like the woman/man you want to eventually become: walk better, talk better, and give yourself credit for the things that you have accomplished!

DO NOT read into someone else's actions. Nowadays people do not have etiquette and their stares or rudeness can be confused as a personal vendetta against you.

DO NOT feel awkward in silence. Sometimes silence is a good thing, it means you are observant and that presents a strong sense of self-confidence.

DO NOT remind those around you that you are a good person and what you do for those you love. If they don't know it, tell them to get lost!

If you are in an intimate relationship, do not emotionally blackmail your companion, making them feel bad for telling the truth, or just being themselves. In your heart you know if they care for you, so don't keep pushing what is obvious or else you will lose them.

YOU HAVE THE RIGHT to present emotions without feeling guilty...However, it must be true and not a distorted delusion of grandeur.

NOTHING IS WRONG WITH YOU...so if someone does not appear to notice you, don't think twice. **IF SOMEONE DOES NOT LIKE YOU**, it is not your fault! Again, they can get lost.

I AGREE WITH THIS PERSONAL FEELING:

Be dependent on you. Don't look to others to validate you, your choices, your values, your morals, your personality, your ideas, and your path. One of the hardest things for me, and something I work on daily, is the thought that I wasn't good enough. I was always afraid to fail. I started to change the way I thought and that changed the way I felt, and the way I saw things.

I do know that there isn't any person in this world that can make me or break me. People can hurt me, they can make me sad, and they can do the things that people do; they just can't break my spirit. I know now that when you turn to others for validation, to prove that you are ok; worthy; useful or whatever, it gives others too much power over you. Everyone struggles with self-esteem because if it was easy everyone would have it, right?

CHAPTER SEVEN

HOW TO BOOST UP YOUR CONFIDENCE

Have you ever wondered why men only get a certain type of girl? Some even turn that into a fetish or a game, in order to cover their inability to connect with other people. It comes down to a problem of confidence. What do women mean when they say they are looking for confidence in men? Or, guys talk about growing balls, man up, do something? All these can be traced to one thing – the need to get or boost confidence.

INNER GAME:

I'm sure many can build up their inner confidence (a.k.a. inner-game) with various techniques, but by far the best way of developing inner game is through competence. Competence stems from having experience; so a so-called womanizer really means someone with experience. Most girls want to be led and what they look for is someone who has the experience; someone who has done it before; someone who knows about other people like her, and ultimately, someone who knows what to do with her.

If you are the adventurous type, talk to a few different girls... maybe even out of your league. The best way to introduce yourself is to talk (ugh, I know, "brag") about yourself. Tell her a story, preferably a funny one; let her know that you have been with girls like her. Of course, if you don't know what kind of girl she is, then start going through your stack of stories with different types of girls. The goal is to communicate that you have experience with girls like her and by inference, you know what to do with her; you can lead.

Some ways to generate stories include:

(1) Be open to new experiences, live an adventurous life.

(2) By proxy, through watching, reading, and talking with others.

(3) Learn to tell stories. Successful guys are ones who don't set their lives to just getting girls. Guys who do become dating coaches; they are better at seducing girls. The next step is to go out, just to mingle and talk with strangers. I, rarely, ever have to game a girl. In fact, keep the interaction light and fun. Game is really necessary once you are in isolation, then you have to slow down the interaction, where you turn from verbal to physical. That's why touching early and often is important.

You don't get the "stop sign" as you transition to physical.

So, grow some balls, man up, and start talking to strangers. Get into the habit of sharing with people. Eventually, you will build up a repertoire of stories, routines, and finally, experience with different types of girls. Why travel the world, when you can make girls from different parts of the world, umm, come to us?!

LOVE IS BLIND. BUT HAVING CONFIDENCE IS FINE.

THE BEST WAY TO AVOID INSECURITIES IS TO HAVE A LOT OF CONFIDENCE, LOOK IN THE MIRROR AND SAY:

I AM WHO I AM AND THAT'S HOW GOD MADE ME.

Now repeat that about five times, take a deep breath in and out, **YOU ARE WHO YOU ARE; ACCEPT IT!** If they don't like it ,fuck 'em. There are so many single people that will like you for you; don't let anyone bring you down.

OVERCONFIDENCE: Cocksure, brash, arrogant, reckless, heedless.

Being overconfident can put a strain on your character. Basically it's a big turn off. You start giving off shade, or a certain aura that can push people away, more than likely leaving you unapproachable. So now you're fly, got money, your swag is on 100 but being overconfidence will give off a cocky aura. Make people feel like you don't need their friendship and make it hard for people who want to get to know you, make that effort.

CHAPTER EIGHT

HOW TO NOT CARE

WHAT PEOPLE THINK

Not caring what other people think isn't easy. It takes a lot of practice and confidence in yourself. Here are some tools to help you:

Understand that the less you care what people think of you, the more they might like you. Why? Because no matter what, people like novelty. People like other people that are different, except when that something different is disrespectful.

Having an eclectic personality sets you apart from other people. Even if someone else has something in common with you, doesn't change the fact that you still have a personality. Other people can have a hard time making friends because, well, they're other people; but not you. So, developing yourself and your personality will give people reasons to talk to you.

Also understand that the more that you show you don't care what people think of you, the less they will like you.

Why? Because no matter how much pressure there seems to be to "not care what people think", people like to be cared about. People dislike other people that make them feel sad, angry, or uncomfortable. Not making someone else sad, angry, or uncomfortable means caring about what they feel. People who don't care about other people have a hard time making friends because, well, friends are other people. So, developing your social skills and your personality gives people a reason to keep talking to you instead of avoiding you.

HERE ARE SOME OF MY SUGGESTIONS:

Learn to accept yourself as is; that's the most important thing!

Think about why others might judge you. What are they like? Are they jealous or even do they like you? If they dislike you; then forget them – they are not worth your time.

Think about why you might be judging other people. Are you envious of them or even attracted to them? You might just have taken a dislike to them. They should ignore you – they should get you out of their lives.

Take a good look at yourself in the mirror and say this aloud: "I am (me). I love myself; accept myself and those who judge my looks will find it harder to know me."

Smile at those who judge you, if you feel like smiling (but don't fake it). Don't smile broadly or it will look like you want them to know something they don't. Just give a relaxed smile. If people see you happy they will think that you have a lot going on.

Don't try to be popular at school/work. If you don't care what people think then there's no reason why you should try to be popular.

Don't complain about becoming unpopular at school/work.

Observe the people that are measuring your actions - don't be afraid to look someone in the eye. Understand how ridiculous their actions are; why are they acting that way? Realize that if you are "worthless" then they are worthless too.

Are you measuring the actions of others - for example, calling them stupid and dull because their outside appearances aren't exciting enough

for you? - don't be afraid if they look you in the eye. Note how ridiculous what you are doing is - why are you acting like that? Realize that if they are "worthless" then you are equally worthless.

Collect yourself. This world is for you, and it is for your neighbors as well, so make the best out of your experiences; instead of putting out the negativity.

Do what you want to do. If you have a phone, instead of texting, write a note to someone. If you like to do crossword puzzles, do some. If you like to do Sudoku, go ahead!

Don't be pretentious. Just because being carefree is necessary for a good life doesn't mean you have to overdo it. For example, when you get the opportunity to make a friend, don't just blow them off because you don't "care what they think" or "the less you care what people think of you, the more they will like you."

Keep a diary. Every time you're feeling down, write a note about it. When you're feeling better you can look back at what was written and think, "How did this make me stronger?"

Do not worry about how you walk or how you appear to others.

Do not worry about how other people walk or how they appear to you.

Once again, DO NOT try to become popular. People can smell desperation from a mile away. If they think you're trying too hard, they will push you around for fun, just to see how far you'll go. Remember, you don't want to become the popular crowd's little bioch, licking their feet and begging to bring them their stuff so that you'll belong.

Don't want anyone else, not even your girlfriend or boyfriend, to become your bioch.

Have faith in yourself. Remember, nobody can take away your faith.

CHAPTER NINE

PRIDE

In today's society a lot of young people have pride but not always pride in things acceptable to society. For example, pride in school-work or graduating high school. Pride is sometimes based on a ride, sneakers or securing a corner.

Pride is defined as a high or inordinate opinion of one's own dignity, importance, merit, or superiority, whether as cherished in the mind or as displayed in bearing, conduct.

The problem with pride is that it can get between you and what you really want. It can stop you from doing what you know is right. It keeps you from asking for help. It can block empathy and make you appear cold and uncaring. It can keep you from happiness because pride will prevent you from finding love and people have been known to sacrifice many things in the name of pride.

So, I would advise swallowing your pride. It's difficult at first, but gets easier with practice. Decide what you really want. Decide what is really important. For example, do you miss a friend? If you still want your friend in your life, tell him (or her). It may not work out, but you will have left the door open to renewing the friendship and it will give you inner-peace in the end.

Pride is something we all have and it could be good but it can also bad.

Have you ever noticed that having so much pride will make you lose someone you love? Your pride will lead you to ignore and forget that you really liked that person. Now you have regrets because of your stupid ass pride. Sometime you have no choice other than to put your pride aside. Don't ask, "When do you know you have to put it aside?" You know, trust me. It's a gut feeling you get when your subconscious talks to you.

For example: You're talking to a woman/man for about a week, everything is going great. Three weeks later, after numerous conversations, you're at a certain comfortable stage. OK, cool; conversation goes a little left and the person says something out of character. Now you can easily ignore it and laugh it off, and in a calm manner say, "I don't like that, it bothers me" but noooooo you want to get all riled up, become argumentative. This is an example of pride getting in the way so put your PRIDE ASIDE.

DO YOU HAVE A CLOSET?
...YES
WELL HANG THIS UP (BANG)

Now you could have simply avoided that by just thinking before you speak. Now in your mind you're going to say "on to the next one," but deep down inside you're hurting cause you have been through this before and it's like a cycle; so it's time for a change.

PUT YOUR PRIDE ASIDE: Putting your pride aside isn't that hard, not hard at all. You just have to put another person's feelings before your own. REGRET is a hell of a thing. When you regret something you tend to beat yourself up about it, not literally, but you get really down on yourself. And we don't need that in our life. Some people will say, "I never did anything that I've regretted." Well I say **SHUT THE FUCK UP**, because when you were a child, and you did something wrong, then got punished, you didn't regret doing it? Now, I bet you are going to say, "Well, I didn't know better -- I was a child." OK then, as an adult, let's say you had to pick a friend up from a party, but changed your mind last minute and something bad happened; now when you feel bad would you say I should have picked him up? EXACTLY. That's a form of regret.

LACK OF COMPASSION IS THE KEY PART IN SELFISHNESS THAT HURTS YOUR RELATIONSHIP

So, I just want you to put your pride aside and take people's feelings into consideration; they will appreciate you.

People with too much pride are actually very vulnerable and scared. The fear behind having too much pride comes from not wanting to appear too needy. Too much pride can destroy any relationship. It would help if you recognize you have a problem with too much pride and to decide if you are willing to do something about it?

The first step is to stop being so scared of being wrong and admitting it. You have to come to believe that saying "I'm sorry" to your boyfriend/girlfriend is not saying you are weak, in fact it says the opposite. It says you are a big enough person to admit when you are wrong and this takes courage. It is important for you to learn to tell the difference between being weak and simply being sorry and admitting it. To say you are sorry does not mean you are begging, it means that you own up to hurting the other person.

All good relationships come with a give and take; compromises. If your boyfriend/girlfriend is the one doing all the giving in the "I'm sorry" department then pretty soon he/she will grow resentful. Why not start breaking the "too much pride" habit by going up to him/her and saying, "**I am so sorry for never apologizing to you all the times when I knew that I was wrong. It is just that I was scared to appear too needy by admitting any wrongdoings on my part. I am willing to make some changes and hope you are willing to give me the chance to do so**". This will be a positive step towards maturity and he/she will admire you for it. After this, take it one step at a time and force the words "**I am sorry**" out when you know you need to say them.

PERSONAL EXPERIENCE

I have a lot of pride issues mainly because I'm always on the defensive. Now if you are reading this and you personally know me, you know I have some pride issues. Pride has fucked up a lot of shit for me in my life. In fact, the woman that I loved, with all my heart, has disowned me because of my pride.

I remember one story off hand: I met this model, well she's a model now, at the time she was in every magazine, every teen event. I was driving a black Pontiac (which I eventually crashed into a house on Dunkirk), that day and for some reason I was extra fly. I rarely got fly; honestly, fashion wasn't my thing back then, it was making money and getting women. Anyway, I saw her, got out of the car and got the number.

I called her the next day and it was on like popcorn. Now I didn't hit it, but let's just say at the movie parking lot in Brooklyn, I had a happy ending by her friend 'palm a la'. Anywho, after that night she told me I can hit it for sure; so a week passed and I was just a little thirsty, honestly, so I called. She stood me up two times, so I flipped; so she told me to calm down and that she was gonna see me the next day. But you know how it go, I played hard to get, saying lines like, "I'm good" or "NAH forget it." But deep down inside I wanted to see her; so she proceeded to tell me to "man up" and stop acting like a little bitch and guess what I did? I could have laughed it off and proceeded but then I turned Flip and cursed her out – THAT WAS MY PRIDE.

A lot of people may not remember when pride first became an issue for them, but I do. My first memory was in 5TH Grade; 1998. I met this girl and it was love at first sight. I won't mention her name but if she reads this she will know it's about her. Now like I said it was love at first sight; man, when I looked at this girl my stomach hurt. You know when you like someone so much, you just mean to them for no reason? Well that's how it was.

62

Now she paid me no attention and I loved it, and loved her more. Honestly, I love her till this day; we are still in contact but she's selfish; I will explain later...

Before this whole pride shit, I was just a class clown. So one day I confessed my love for this young lady and she acted liked she cared, but I overheard her tell someone else that I was annoying – just a little pest, and that shit crushed me. So from then on, I always felt someone would try to play me, so my pride and defense are always high.

CHAPTER TEN

FRAUDULENT A.K.A. FRONTIN

Are you fraudulent, a frontier? Do you think frontin is going to get you what you want? Well it ain't, cause frontin is a bitch.

Definition: A person or thing that serves as a cover or disguise for some other activity, esp. one of a secret, disreputable, or illegal nature; a blind; a façade, considered with respect to its material.

Frontin is what most of us have trouble overcoming these days; trying to live up to everyone's expectations. In most situations fraudulent behavior becomes part of our daily routine. Some wake up frontin; go to sleep frontin; make frontin part of our everyday activity. People that front in my opinion are basically trying to live up to everyone's expectations. I bet if you ask 99% of the fronters they will tell you that is how they are but that's bullshit.

First of all it's some of the parents' fault that leads the teens or young adults to front. If you live in the projects and/or on Section 8 (by the way there's nothing wrong with either) you will have a little extra money because the government pays half, so the rent isn't a lot. Now with that extra money, you will buy clothing and extra stuff that isn't necessary for your survival. Now you go to school or the hood, and portray to the world as if you are getting it, but in reality your parent just took advantage of the system. Now if someone put your ass on blast, you will get upset. My main point is to stay humble and everything will be all right.

Another form of Frontin is if you're getting money in the streets, and then you want to be a badass, "gangster"; fight n shit. It's impossible, if you're not a real hustler to get money and deal with beef at the same time: 1. You'll be so nervous that you wouldn't even feel comfortable getting it. Now you're going to say, "What does this have to do with relationships?" Well, if you front and your significant other finds out the real you, not only would they leave you but they will also tarnish your name. 2. Since you're scared, eventually it limits your clientele.

It is like a guy who brags about their penis size; seven times out of ten the guys are over exaggerating. To females it might sound good but when they put you through the test and you fail. Oh boy! If you build an image of yourself and you get a person that likes you for that image then they see that isn't you, what do you think they'll do?

PERSONAL EXPERIENCE:

I was caught frontin numerous times but I stopped at an early age. You see, getting caught in frontin is an embarrassment. Trust me, I fronted about shit. Like I remember I was in the "Pump It Up Video". I had my cousin charger, when they first came out on 24/7 – lol. Anyway I thought I was POPPPPPPIN.

He let me hold the car for the day, so I went to the mall and did what we call 'parking lot pimpin'. So I meet someone, kick it off instantly. We made plans to go to the telly later on that night (I WAS 17). So I pick her up later and we went to the telly about 8p.m. Now Ima bout to smash but my cousin kept calling my jack, so I told her I gotta go cause of an emergency.

So I dropped the car off and then stayed in the mansion. My cousin goes off with the ride; I'm stranded in this big ass house and no boonkie (meaning pussy). About two hours past, guess who my cousin came back to the mansion with? Yup, that same chick. Now you gonna say, well why didn't

66

you bring her to the mansion in the first place; I was given specific orders to bring no one to the mansion.

So he humpin her and her friend and then call me to go to the store. She sees me get into the side seat and started laughing, so I'm like what's so funny you're the same bitch I just fucked, then she called me 2 Slips Flip- LOL- and exposed me. Now can you figure out how I fronted? I acted like the car was mine and I fronted to a jump off.

CHAPTER ELEVEN

MAKING A GREAT FIRST IMPRESSION!

Instead of frontin to get a girl's attention, work on your image; make a great first impression. It takes just a quick glance, maybe three seconds, for someone to evaluate you when you meet for the first time. In this short time, the other person forms an opinion about you based on your appearance, body language, demeanor and mannerisms.

With every new encounter, you are evaluated and another impression of you is formed. These first impressions can be nearly impossible to undo; therefore, make those first encounters important, because they set the tone for the relationship that follows.

So, whether it is in your career or social life, it's important to know how to create a good first impression.

Be on Time

The person you are meeting for the first time is not interested in your "excuse" for running late. Plan to arrive a few minutes early and allow flexibility for possible delays in traffic or taking a wrong turn. Arriving early is much better than arriving late, hands down, and is the first step in creating a great first impression.

Be Yourself, Be at Ease

If you are feeling uncomfortable and on edge, this can make the other person feel uneasy and that's a sure way to create the wrong impression. If you are calm and confident, the other person will feel more at ease, and you will have a solid foundation for making that first impression.

Present Yourself Appropriately

Of course physical appearance matters. The person you are meeting for the first time does not know you and your appearance is usually the first clue he or she has to go on. But it certainly does not mean you need to look like a model to create a strong and positive first impression. Unless you are interviewing with your local model agency, of course! No. The key to a good impression is to present yourself appropriately.

They say a picture is worth a thousand words, and so the "picture" you first present says much about you to the person you are meeting. Ask yourself, is your appearance saying the right things to help create the right first impression?

Start with the way you dress. What is the appropriate dress for the meeting or occasion? In a business setting, what is the appropriate business attire? Suit, blazer, casual? Ask yourself what the person you'll be meeting is likely to wear - if your contact is in the music industry, a business suit may not strike the right note!

For business and social meetings, appropriate dress also varies between countries and cultures, so it's something that you should pay particular attention to when you are in an unfamiliar setting or country. Make sure you know the traditions and norms.

Also, what about your personal grooming? Clean and tidy appearance is appropriate for most business and social occasions. A good haircut or shave. Clean and tidy clothes. Neat and tidy make-up. Make sure your grooming is appropriate and helps make you feel "the part". Being appropriately dressed also helps you feel calm and confident.

A Word about Individuality

You do not need to totally conform or lose your individuality to make a good first impression but you do have to fit in to some degree. This goes back to being appropriate for the situation. If in a business setting, wear appropriate business attire. If it's a formal evening social event, wear appropriate evening attire. Express your individuality appropriately within that context.

A Winning Smile!

"Smile and the world smiles too."* So there's nothing like a smile to create a good first impression. A warm and confident smile will put both you and the other person at ease. So smiling is a winner when it comes to great first impressions. But don't go overboard with it - people who take this too far can seem insincere and smarmy, or can be seen as "lightweights".

71

Be Open and Confident

When it comes to making the first impression, body language as well as appearance speaks much louder than words. Use your body language to project appropriate confidence and self-assurance. Stand tall, smile (of course), make eye contact, greet with a firm handshake. All of this will help you project confidence and help both you and the other person to feel at ease.

Almost everyone gets a little nervous when meeting someone for the first time, which can lead to nervous habits or sweaty palms. By being aware of your nervous habits, you can try to keep them in check. And controlling a nervous jitter or a nervous laugh will give you confidence and help the other person feel at ease.

Small Talk Goes a Long Way...

Conversations are based on verbal give and take. It may help you to prepare questions you have for the person you are meeting for the first time beforehand. Or, take a few minutes to learn something about the person you are meeting for the first time before you get there; for instance, does he play basketball? Does she work at a bank?

Is there anything you have in common with the person you are meeting? If so, this can be a great way to open the conversation and to keep it flowing.

Be Positive

Your attitude shows through in everything you do. Project a positive attitude, even in the face of criticism or in the case of nervousness. Strive to learn from your meeting and to contribute appropriately, maintaining an upbeat manner and a smile.

Be Courteous and Attentive

It goes without saying that good manners and polite, attentive and courteous behavior help make a good first impression. In fact, anything less can ruin the one chance you have at making that dynamite first impression. So be on your best behavior!

One modern foible worth mentioning is "turn off your mobile phone". What first impression will you create if you answer the call and start speaking to someone other than the person you are meeting for the first time? Your new acquaintance deserves 100% of your attention; anything less and you'll create a less than stellar first impression.

Key Points

You have just a few seconds to make a good first impression and it's almost impossible to ever change it. So it's worth giving each new encounter your best shot. Much of what you need to do to make a good impression is common sense. But with a little extra thought and preparation, you can hone your intuitive style and make every first impression not just good but great.

CHAPTER TWELVE

DEFENSIVENESS

Now I have a lot to say about defensiveness, that's one of MY MAIN PROBLEMS, so I found an article that I read so that I can better understand what this word means and to see if it applies to me. I had to research this because honestly I don't want to admit I have an anger issue, which in turn led me to be defensive. So I did some research from one of my father's books, he's a health doctor, an herbalist, no not weed; predominantly he deals with herbs and helps heal people. So if you don't want to read what I researched, go to the next chapter, because a lot of us have a defensive problem and we need help.

1. **Domination of Others**. This means that the individual is being dominated by another who has more control. For example, forcing others to write one's letter will compensate for one's inability to read and write. The Dominator thinks if they fail, the others would learn their fatal flaw, and could take advantage of it. Obviously, dominating others is usually not the same as working toward your own objective.

2. **Winning at all Costs.** Is another defense to compensate for an individual's lack of

control; they must win against all others. This defensive need to compete is the opposite of cooperation within the group. Because of this, an individual is driven to look good, and always must somehow create the perception of being superior to others.

3. **Being Right.** Compensation tied to the defense of needing to win and is the need to be right at all costs.

4. **Possessiveness.** Compulsive possessiveness is another substitute for lack of control. Here the individual clings to the supports of significant possessions, positions of power, even relationships, in an attempt to avoid falling out of control.

5. **Trying to Change Things.** Another compensation for failure to control an operation is the attempt to improve an approach that already doesn't work, by applying different ways of accomplishing the change.

CHAPTER THIRTEEN

DECEPTION

Cheating in a relationship is such a norm today that I don't know if there is such a thing as a monogamous couple; especially in my age group.

Deception is a trick, stratagem, ruse, wile, hoax, imposture.

Dealing with Lying and Cheating:

Initially, most people think about the topic of lying and infidelity after a recent experience. For better or for worse romantic relationships are not always as straightforward. There are times when intimate relationships can become complicated and complex. When it comes to love and marriage, people expect their significant other to be completely honest. But, at the same time, everyone values their sense of freedom and privacy. So while partners typically want to please each other, at other times, they experience competing goals which makes telling the truth difficult. As it stands, close relationships involve truth telling as well as dishonesty. If love were straightforward and unchanging then it would be easy. But, when you take a close look at the nature of love and romance, one thing becomes clear: Love creates both happiness and heartache, opportunities and constraints, joy and sorrow. At times spouses are considerate, honest and kind. But at the same time they will betray their loved ones.

Deception comes in handy when an individual want to limit their partner's choices, avoid conflict or punishment, or when they want to influence their partner's behavior. While it is not uncommon for people to lie and cheat, it is difficult to accept that one's own husband or wife might be doing it. So who hasn't caught a boyfriend or girlfriend lying only to have him or her deny it - "I would never lie to you." Not only can close relationships cause heartache and anxiety, but it's also difficult to discuss lying and cheating out in the open. When you mention the possibility that love and betrayal might go hand-in-hand, people tend to get angry or they become defensive.

Deceivers:

Now deception is hell, or should I say being deceived. Everyone knows that being deceived is one of the most hurtful things in a relationship. But have you ever asked yourself as the deceiver why do I go through all of that, just to be back into the same situation? The reason I say "back in the same situation" is because once you get caught, nine times out of ten your loved one is going to leave you.

A lot of us deceive one another to get what we want in life; we will pretend to like someone because we are materialistic and want things. Think about it, you're dating someone who you know deep down you don't give two shits about, but you know this person's capabilities are substantial.

So what do we do? We tell them what they want to hear, we use all the power within our ability just to make this person do more and more and more. Is it because we like them? NOOOOOOOOO. You and I both know that we don't give two shits about that person. Now I don't discriminate because who am I to judge, but a lot of you go too far, way too far. My main problem is if you're going to have your "JOINT trick" or whatever don't disrespect them by doing shit in their house or car, and also by throwing it in their face. Try to have respect, now I don't condone deception but it is what it is.

Deceived:

Now to the one that gets deceived, you and I both know, you know you're being deceived. Unless the person you mess with is a personal assistant to James Bond, you can tell. Is your self-esteem that low that you need someone to control you, and your personal beliefs? Ask yourself that. You mean to tell me, you didn't notice that every time you wanted to do something, the deceiver stands you up. You didn't notice that every time they're in a bad situation, they call you, no matter how long you guys haven't spoken. They call you and what do you do, huh? What do you do, say it with me:_ **I IGNORE THE FACT I'M GETTING PLAYED AND GO RUNNING BACK TO THEM.** Exactly! So we have no one else to blame but ourselves. Sometimes we put ourselves in a black hole that secludes us from the people that can keep it real with us. We either think they're hating or they don't want to see us happy, but that's not always the case. Always trust in yourself, and your inner feelings. Don't doubt yourself at all.

I have a saying, **WHEN YOU'RE HEART SAYS NO AND YOUR INNER THOUGHTS (SUBCONSCIOUS) SAYS YES, FOLLOW YOUR SUBCONSCIOUS OR VICE VERSA.** There is a difference and I am going to break it down for you. Someone cheats on you (you actually saw them with your own two eyes). Now a couple of weeks pass by, and they are begging for your forgiveness, practically on their hands and knees. Your heart yearns to take them back, BUT your subconscious says no because it'll happen again. Now half of you would take them back for numerous reasons. For example, some would say they don't feel like starting all over; they don't want to go through the hassle. Others would just blame it on love.

My former teacher Mrs. Moore would say that these are excuses and **EXCUSES ARE THE TOOLS FOR THE WEAK AND INCOMPETENT; THEY BUILD AND LEAD BRIDGES TO NOWHERE.** Now I don't want to misinterpret the point, but the message I got was you can lie to yourself but the truth is the truth. You can keep making excuses in order to satisfy your personal feelings but at the end of the day you will come to a realization that all your excuses were a bunch of crock. You can read between the lines, we as people put ourselves through some dumb shit.

CHAPTER FOURTEEN

CLINGY

Do you have a sense that your girlfriend or boyfriend restricts your lifestyle with excessive neediness, jealousy, controlling behavior, or by being too demanding? A relationship is a place to build something -- both partners should help the other have a better life. Compromises need to be made, but each person should not have the sense that they are tied down by neediness, jealousy, etc. If your relationship is more like a hostage situation than a healthy relationship, you may need relationship help fast.

Your relationship may be unhealthy if your partner:

- Demands to be by your side all the time;
- Expects you to call several times a day;
- Needs to know where you're going at all times;
- Shows jealousy over your normal interactions with others;
- Ticked off at you having friends of the opposite sex.
- Discourages you from spending time with male friends

- Has you walking on eggshells for fear of "slipping up"
- Demands to analyze everything about your relationship
- Pressures you to make commitments when you're not ready, such as marriage
- Acts clingy in public or too protective

You may be accustomed to their behaving like this and you might accept that it's just the way it is. It's your choice if you wish to maintain a relationship with someone who acts like this, but it's important to be aware of these behaviors – they're signs of an unhealthy relationship. When one partner is controlling or unstable, the other partner often experiences negative physical and mental effects from the stress. A lifetime of tolerating this behavior is a miserable existence.

A partner who acts clingy, needy, or excessively jealous tends to have major self-esteem issues. Since people tend to pair-off with partners with similar levels of self-esteem, you may have such issues of your own. You can address your own self-esteem issues later, but first, you must determine if your partner's level of neediness, jealousy, etc., is something you wish to address.

In a healthy relationship, each partner is comfortable bringing up problems, so address these issues with your partner if you're able to do so. Let your partner know that you are feeling boxed-in because of the way they try to hold tightly to the relationship. Tell him/her that a sense of freedom and independence is important to you, and you're not feeling that because their behavior is affecting you.

For example, many men in relationships with controlling women feel uncomfortable bringing up issues. In fact, they're afraid of discussing things with their partner because she may overreact or respond in a way that causes more disruption. If you wish to stay in the relationship, you may need to discuss your issues with a third party, in a setting where you know you can speak your mind without fear of negative consequences.

What if you have don't want to maintain this relationship? Do you have the sense that you want to leave your partner but it is just not the right time? A birthday is coming up, a parent who is ill, you just can't leave her now in her time of need. The truth is, there is never a good time to leave, and if you think you're staying for their benefit, you're wrong. You're wasting their time (and yours).

So many men stay with controlling women because they can't find the strength to leave. The man wants out, but several reasons keep him in the relationship:

- He doesn't want to hurt her
- He fears that she won't be able to handle the break up and will do something drastic
- He can't stand to see her cry
- He's scared that she will go berserk, and may try to ruin both their lives
- She relies on him for a place to live, a ride to work, etc.
- They have a common lease, dog, etc.
- They are engaged and the family and friends expect a wedding

There are many more reasons why you might feel stuck in an unhealthy relationship, but they usually have the same theme in common: You feel responsible for her, can't stand hurting her, and feel that she may not be able to handle life without you. These are not good reasons to stay in a relationship. If this is you, you need to <u>leave the relationship</u> now.

You don't have to be in a relationship to be clingy; once you give off a clingy aura, calling excessively or always underneath a person at a party, these key factors turn people away.

PERSONAL EXPERIENCE

Now I had a tendency of being clingy, a lot of girls cut me off on that nonsense. But that wasn't my intention at all. I just like progression and I also like things to be on point. Like the person I mentioned earlier; the one from 5TH grade. Well, I recently (OK not so recent) had another chance and I knew that she was in a situation but love is love; right? It's like when she's around me I feel crazy. I didn't call that much but I was so mushy and shit. Like WTF I wasn't her man; LOL. Anyway, I say give people their space and you'll get far that's all; not too much space but just enough.

CHAPTER FIFTEEN

CHEATING

Now some of you reading this will be mad because this describes you down to the bone; everyone cheats, whether it's innocent or not we all cheat but there are different kinds of cheaters:

The flirtatious cheaters: The one that will do inappropriate things in front of you, for instance, bend over in front of you, or eat a candy in a prerogative way but would never go 3rd base.

The honest cheaters: The ones who let you know from the gate that they got a hubby or wifey and you can't get within 200 miles of their significant other, they'll even discuss their personal problems with their side joint.

The Cry Cheaters: The ones that have sex with you, and call out their significant other's name, in an apologetic tone, even go as far as saying sorry to them, aloud. They also cry while performing sexual acts on you.

The Grimy Cheater: Now they cheat with no remorse whatsoever. Will usually have no respect for their partner and will have sex with your mother, father, brother, sister, anyone - ruthless.

Now we all have temptation, but controlling that temptation is the key to a successful relationship. I have gathered 9 reasons to why people cheat.

1. **Bored:** I'd say this is the most common reason that people cheat. Things start off great, then level off and then you both realize that it's real life. When you meet someone else that adds excitement in your life, makes you feel different than your significant other; a new relationship will automatically kick in.

2. **Dependence:** At first glance, cheating seems like independent behavior. It could be interpreted as doing what you want, when you want. But I would argue that cheating is a dependent behavior. A cheater is dependent because they are not strong enough to break up with their partner in order to get with the new person.

3. **Confusion:** Sometimes life or a particular situation can get to you. When the perfect storm of confusion is going on in your head, you make mistakes.

4. **Because they let you:** If any girl ever cheated on me, I'd break up with her immediately. Forgiving a cheater is putting up with it, and starts a vicious cycle. That person who cheated may lose respect for you and might continue to cheat because they know they can get away with it; you'll continue to take them back.

5. **Nurturing:** If someone is mistreating you, then your first instinct is to get away from him or her. But sometimes it's not that simple-maybe you are raising kids together. If you feel trapped in a bad relationship, it's only natural that you will run to the open arms of a person who treats you right.

6. **Revenge:** This is quite simple- "an eye for an eye". Cheat on them if they cheat on you. If they continuously hurt you or abuse you in some way, you do it to get them back.

7. **Confirmation of Attractiveness:** Sometimes when you're in a long relationship, or if your significant other is taking you for granted, you begin to wonder if you're still attractive. Perhaps, because you were out on the dating circuit, you felt more attractive when you were single. If you have an affair, you've proven that a new person can be attracted to you.

8. **The Thrill:** Some people just enjoy the thrill of cheating: running around secretly, risking getting caught, and creating with a forbidden romance.

9. **They don't consider it Cheating; Even Though You Might:** Relationships have that gray area, usually right before you become exclusive. He thinks date #4 is when you're "together," and you think date #2 is when you're "together." If you haven't talked about exclusivity, someone may think they are well within their rights to see other people, even though the other person in the relationship may not.

I don't understand why people don't break up as soon as they have an urge to cheat. I wonder is it natural to have temptation, or is temptation a sign that the relationship is losing its fire? What reasons would you add to this list, and do you disagree with any? If you've ever cheated, why did you do it? Could you forgive a cheater? If you are single, but seeing a person who is in a committed relationship, does that make you a cheater?

Open your eyes:

The problem is that sometimes people are quick to point the finger at others rather than analyze why the individual cheated. Maybe your own actions had a big role in pushing the other to the brink of temptation. By blaming and labeling others, it inevitably hinders people from looking deeper into the problem and trying to resolve it before it happens with another partner. The common belief is: I'm not a bad person. I don't need to change; I'm not the one who cheated. The result is that the whole process repeats itself without being rectified, which is probably why so many men and women complain about having been cheated on in so many relationships.

I'm going to give you the top 10 excuses that someone gives when they are caught cheating

1. I don't love you anymore.

2. It's not you, it's me.

3. I need some space.

4. You deserve better.

5. We were just friends.

6. You don't listen to me.

7. You don't need me.

8. I'm having a mid-life crisis.

9. I can't help myself.

10. It doesn't mean anything.

Now that you are aware, even though you were aware of the shenanigans from the get go, what will you do? Remember, CHEATERS NEVER PROSPER.

Before I end this chapter, I'm going to elaborate an issue that bothers me. And that issue is ACCEPTANCE. I hate with a passion a woman or man, who accepts their significant other's cheating ways, and instead of cutting them off, they will continue to make excuses and excuses, saying lines like, "Look where he's at now." Or, "At least he's home in my bed every night." Ok, that's cool but you sound like a shallow ass. This is where your pride needs to kick in; once you accept negativity you are subjected to future negativity.

CHAPTER SIXTEEN

JERKS AND WHY THEY ACHIEVE MORE

It is a proven fact that Jerks get more love than the nice guy. I don't know why, but that's how life is. For example, society is so backwards because a nice guy will wait patiently, and most females always tell the nice guy they're not ready, etc. But once they see a Jerk, or a guy with more confidence, they give it up way faster than they would for the nice guy. Then they run to the nice guy when they get played. Is that right? Why should the nice guy get that treatment? Me personally I am a Jerk, but I realize that it's wrong how the nice guy gets treated. So for those of you who don't understand I have a breakdown method for you.

1. **Jerks are self-centered**

   One of the big things a Jerk has going for him is that he really doesn't care about other people. In fact, his focus is almost entirely on his own pleasures, thoughts, and feelings. Because of this, when he sees something he wants, he goes after it!

When your average "nice guy" sees a hot girl, he might be intimidated. He wants her to like him. He wants approval from her. In short – he cares about what she thinks!

In addition to that he cares about what others think too! He worries about a girl rejecting him in front of other people, and what people will think when this happens.

Jerks do not have this problem. They couldn't care less about what other people think. A Jerk is only focused on getting what he wants.

When you allow yourself to focus on your goals, and set aside fears of judgment from others, this gives you a great deal of focus, and as we all know, focus is key to achieving what we desire.

2. **Jerks aren't afraid to approach women**

The single, most important step in getting a woman is walking up and talking to her.

94

So many guys just DON'T DO THIS. They are too shy or too intimidated by the girl to do so. Instead, they hang back and just stare at her like a big dummy, wishing he could find the balls to meet her.

Jerks don't hesitate to approach a girl. They're not worried about whether or not she's going to like them, because THEY DON'T CARE.

They're thinking about how hot it's going to be to make out with her. They're thinking about how much fun it will be to get her in bed. The LAST thing on their mind is "fear of rejection." To a Jerk, if a girl rejects him, there's something wrong with HER, not him. Nice guys will say, "Oh, I'm too ugly, she doesn't like me." Jerks will say, "That bitch is a total lesbian."

Just the act of being able to approach a girl and start talking to her puts the Jerk at an advantage, because he's interacting with the girl and the "nice guy" isn't. To the girl, the nice guy doesn't exist. That's why women typically have such low opinions of men, because it's always the Jerks who are approaching the women while the shy guys sit off in the corner!

Jerks realize it's not the woman's job to approach the guy. If you want something, you have to go after it. So if the nice guys were to start walking up and talking to women, they might be surprised to find most women want their company because they really want to meet a good guy to treat them right.

3. **Jerks don't censor themselves**

Part of the reason Jerks come off as fun, interesting, or exciting is because they aren't worried about offending anybody. They will talk about whatever, joke about whatever, and even broach "sensitive" topics of conversation without a blink of an eye.

Too many "nice guys" hold back when they talk to a girl they like. They never bring up sex. They don't even joke about it. Hell, they don't even show any sign they even like the girl and because of this, the Nice Guys become the Boring Guys.

The Jerk will come along, make a joke, tell the girl a nasty story, and even make fun of the girl! He could care less if he offends somebody. To the Jerk, he's just doing what comes naturally to him. Attitude like this is sometimes like a breath of fresh air to many women, because they mistake it as "confidence." But the more they are around the Jerk, the more they realize it isn't confidence at all – it's just narcissism, and a complete lack of caring about others.

A nice guy would do well to "loosen up" when first meeting a girl and not try and please her so much, just like the Jerk does. But in the long run, it's okay to care about what a girl thinks and be on your best behavior. But do this ONLY after you've got her attention.

4. **Jerks are honest about what they want.**

When a Jerk approaches a woman, he gives no doubt about what he's after. He flirts with her, lusts after her, and tries to convince her to come home and have sex with him. The girl knows right away what the Jerk wants, and after he's made it clear, it is up to her to decide if she wants to give it to him. If not, the Jerk moves on and finds another girl. If so, then the Jerk takes her by the hand and drags her off.

This type of honesty is actually appreciated by women. In contrast, you have the nice guys who try another approach -- they try being an asexual "friend." He hangs out, listens to the girl's problems, tries to help her when she needs it, and then all of a sudden, he springs the fact on

her that he's deeply in love! And the girl
FREAKS.

The reason for this is that the "nice guy," in
trying to not get rejected, misrepresented
himself and has basically built a relationship
with the girl based on lies. Now, the girl has
listed him as a "friend."

So when the guy wants to be more than friends?
The girl feels betrayed, because she's become
accustomed to thinking of him in a certain way,
and now he's demanding she look at him
differently. Not surprisingly, shortly after this
happens, most girls even stop being friends with
the guy!

Nice guys should make their intentions clear
from the start. Flirt with a girl, let her know you
like her and want to date her! If she rejects you,
move on until you find a girl who likes what you
have to offer.

That's what the Jerks do, and it works out great
for them!

5. **Jerks safeguard their self esteem**

All too often, getting rejected by one girl will send a "nice guy" down a well of depression. His self-esteem will hit rock bottom, and he'll get depressed and withdraw for the rest of the night. Jerks don't suffer from this problem. They safeguard their self-esteem and don't allow rejection to get them down.

This is why Jerks are Jerks! Because they will completely ignore rejection, and even go so far as to put down and ridicule other people to make them feel more important than they actually are. This constant guarding of their self-esteem allows them to keep pursuing their goals by not allowing them to fall into the same well as the nice guy. And no matter how you cut it – a guy with high self-esteem is always more attractive to women than a depressed loser.

For the average nice guy, it's important not to take rejection personally. If a girl isn't into you, it doesn't mean you're not attractive, or cool, or interesting – it just means that girl isn't right for you! So you keep looking for one that is, and you don't stop until you find her.

Rejection can be a hard thing for anyone to deal with but remember to keep a positive outlook.

Instead of seeing it as "losing a girl," think of it like "I just eliminated a girl who would have wasted my time."

You don't need to ridicule or bad mouth others to feel good about yourself like Jerks do, but you should protect your self-esteem as viciously as possible, because that will keep you going.

Understand – picking up women is a numbers game. The more women you meet, the more likely it is you'll get one! Jerks succeed due to their tenacity and ability to play the numbers. Nice guys go for one or two women a night while Jerks hit up 20-30.

CHAPTER SEVENTEEN

WOMEN ARE ATTRACTED TO WHAT THEY CAN NOT HAVE

Women want what does not belong to them:

In the Bible it is written that the first woman Eve was thrown out of Paradise – The Garden of Eden - because she ate an apple that she was told she could not eat. From this beginning it is said that women want what doesn't belong to them; including men. Here are some reasons why:

•   They think men in relationship are safer sexually and financially.

•   They think men in relationship are better lovers.

•   They think they will be good boyfriends and take care of them because they take care of their girlfriends.

- They think they've won if they took another girl's man; especially if the guy gave them a hard time in the first place.

2

What does # 2 mean?

It means chicks on the side/ or dude on the side.

But since I am a male, I'm going to give you a male's definition of #2 (no offense):

1. The chick on the side is that girl or woman that gives you what you're lacking at home or with your current significant other (main chick).

   - The chick on the side's duties may include but are not limited to: wild kinky sex, letting you vent out frustrations you may not want to with your main chick, keeping a low profile, understanding that she is not the main chick and can be dropped at any time with no explanation, being on call even if she hasn't heard from her lover in weeks or months.

2. A woman you have good times with, but have no serious commitment to.

3. A woman who will never have her lover's full respect, time or attention. In short someone who

needs good sex and lies to herself in saying "I'm getting' mine..." yeah right. You're confused, girl.

4. Also known as a "jump off" .

Personally, if you're satisfied with the number 2 position by all means, but always remember if you ever make it to the wifey position the same thing will happen to you.

CHAPTER EIGHTEEN
SEXUAL PARTNERS

A lot of people lie about the amount of sexual partners they've had in their lives. Ok, maybe, not people our age but give yourself a few years and it might change. People lie for different reasons because it seems to be one of the most asked questions in a relationship. But why ask, when deep down inside you don't want to know the truth, or can't handle it?

Before you ask you should know that people have different morals and standards, and were raised in different environments. So some people think it's perfectly acceptable and normal to have 21 sexual partners at the age of 25, and there's nothing you can say or do to change their views, because it's normal to them. Some people think the number should be 1.

Why should there be a limit? I think it's unfair that society judges women and men differently on this. If it's okay for a man to be promiscuous then it should be the same for a woman.

I think if a woman is a "slut" for having had x amount of lovers then so shall a man be called a "slut" for x amount of lovers. I don't know what the average amount of sexual partners is, or what is considered "normal." I think very young women are probably different than older women. But I say who cares? This question can only be answered after all the variables have been laid out.

Amount of sexual partners depends on religious beliefs, moral beliefs, sex drive, age, and unfortunately appearance. It is fair to say that two women with the same morals, religion and sex drives could still have a different number of partners based on looks. There is no point in assigning a number as a "should"; for some people one is right and for others, 50. In most Western countries, six as a lifetime average is common. But this is supposed to be the statistic, not a life rule.

Just because your new guy doesn't share your opinions on sexual partners doesn't make him a bad person, nor does it mean he loves you any less. Besides, if you want to get technical, think of all the tricks he could teach you. ;-)

Just my opinion, ladies, besides why do we have sex? For a nut (orgasm)? Do half of you reading this book know what an orgasm is? Well, I'm going give you my definition and what I researched; later.

MEN

A lot of guys are sexually promiscuous when they are young. Then they grow up and want to settle down. If that is the only thing that you have against him, let it go and move forward. He was truthful with you. Far too many women don't make it safe for their men to be truthful with them so they start lying to them.

The answer is if he is serious about you and willing to give up his whoring ways, you need to get over it or it will kill the relationship. He will regret telling you the truth, and NEVER EVER THROW IT IN HIS FACE ESPECIALLY WHEN YOU ARE ANGRY. He invested trust in you and you are not dealing with it appropriately if you criticize his past life.

Don't get offended, ladies, because I have a long sheet on you and not on the men, I'm not too interested in the male species – lol. The female species is what I love to dominate (lol), no - but the female species intrigues me so that's why I have so much to say, and I'm a male.

PERSONAL EXPERIENCE – ADVICE

I HAVE TO WRITE THIS BECAUSE TWO DAYS AGO MY HOME GIRL ASKED ME IF HER VAGINA WILL BECOME LOOSE IF SHE HAS SEX WITH A LOT OF PARTNERS. I TOLD HER

Yes, your vagina can become loose, if you have a lot of sex with "large" men. Generally speaking, your vagina will adapt to the size of your partner's member and if you have frequent sex with large or larger than average men then your vagina will adapt to their size. Also the vagina of a 30 year old woman who is sexually active is probably not going to be as tight as a 17 year old virgin.

1. *The same applies for anal sex; frequent anal sex will loosen the muscles of the anus and make it easier to penetrate.*

2. *It probably will become looser, depending on how many times you have intercourse, but there is a chance that it will most likely become tight if you stop for a little while. How long, it depends on the person.*

3. *It won't become "loose" as in flappy-loose. Sex may feel a little more comfortable, since your body is used to it, but don't worry about your vagina becoming "loose". The vagina is quite flexible, and can "tighten".*

4. Of course!!! Having a lot of sex will definitely make you become loose; especially, if your partners are bigger than you, it will adapt to their size. But if you stop having sex for a while, it may tighten-up again.

In some instances your vagina can become loose (child birth) but not usually. Having sex should actually tighten your vagina unless you're letting someone TOO big stretch you out. When you have sex you should tighten your vaginal muscles, like you are holding in pee. This will exercise those (Kegal) muscles, tightening them. Also it will make your vagina feel tighter during sex. Like the rest of your body, if you exercise your vagina then the muscles will get stronger and you can tighten it.

CHAPTER NINETEEN

WHAT IS AN ORGASM?

Some therapist defined it as "an explosive discharge of neuromuscular tension". There are other definitions, but the word 'tension' comes up in most.

What happens in the body?

According to my research here is the technical stuff that creates orgasm.

- The heart pumps faster and your breathing gets heavier to fuel tensing muscles.

- Hormones such as endorphins and oxytocin are pumped round your brain and body, telling you this is fun.

- Blood is pumped to your genitals to create the tension that will trigger a pudenda reflex (muscular spasm of the genitals).

- That reflex will result in your pelvic-floor muscles contracting between five and 15 times at 0.8-second intervals. This is an orgasm as we know it.

What an orgasm isn't

An orgasm should never be the objective of sex. You can have fun with a partner, feeling aroused, sensual, intimate and loving, and not have an orgasm. Yes, it's fun - but unless you're trying to get pregnant it shouldn't be your primary goal. You can't make someone have an orgasm. What you can do, besides physically stimulating your partner, is create a safe, comfortable and caring environment for them in which an orgasm might happen.

Orgasm is not limited to the genitals; some people can experience orgasm without their genitals being touched. Some people describe the sensation as a "tingle"; for others the feelings go all over the body.

Faking it

Why do some people - male and female - fake orgasms? Some people want to stop sex because their mind or body doesn't want an orgasm. Other people who fake it do it to please their partner. They feel they're letting them down if they don't have an orgasm. Experts say instead of pretending, try and create a relationship where, if you're not in the mood you just say so.

Quality not quantity

Many say that society makes a huge fuss about orgasms. A lot of articles that are written about enhancing your sex life focus on improving orgasms or having more of them. But the intensity of an orgasm is not sexual satisfaction. If you want a good orgasm, you can do it yourself. If you want a satisfying sexual relationship, you'll need a lot more.

In psychosexual therapy, people are told about the 2-6-2 rule. Out of every ten times you have sex, the chances are that twice it'll be fantastic and mind-blowing, and the earth will move; six times it'll be nice but nothing special; and twice you'll wish you hadn't bothered.

CHAPTER TWENTY

GETTING OVER LOVING SOMEONE WHO DOESN'T LOVE YOU

Be honest with yourself. Sometimes, someone with a broken heart needs to recognize that the relationship is over and to decide to stop pursuing this person as they are unable to love in return. To do this however, first ask yourself what might be in his head or his heart; it takes two people to be in a relationship and even though you feel that way doesn't mean your partner feels the same way, so:

• Decide that you need and deserve better.

• Know that you are the most important person and you need to feel good about yourself.

• Be patient, a good person will come into your life and make you happy.

- You can't make someone love you; you have to let them go. If it was meant to be, they will return.

- Try not to contact the person once the relationship is over; hang out with your friends and family. Keep busy.

- Give yourself time to be depressed and get over the loss, but do it in a healthy way.

PERSONAL EXPERIENCE

You know it's hard to go through this shit, especially, when you love someone unconditionally - when she needs you wherever and whenever you always are there. You try to protect her, but she pushes you away. When all her friends left her, you were still there for her but she never really liked you "that way", she always thought of you as her best friend. When you tell her how much you like her, she gets mad at you; you get no love in return from her but you still love her so much. That feeling sucks; it hurts so badly. Especially when there are so many girls that do like you, and want to be with you, but all you want is her...to this point there should be an end. So in my case, I decided to forget her and move on to find someone worth my love, to find someone to really care of me, treat me better and love me.

This applies to me mostly, remember that girl I was writing about earlier in the book? Well, like I said, recently I tried to light the flame for the first time in years. (By the way this is when me and my child's mother were broken up) I tried my best but I didn't achieve anything. She said the feeling was mutual but she was in a situation. Oh well, we will see in my next book – HERE IS A SNEAK PEEK: ANGER IN A RELATIONSHIP.

CHAPTER TWENTY-ONE

ANGER IN A

RELATIONSHIP

Anger in a relationship is a very dangerous thing. It can cause a lot of damage to a relationship. It consists of verbal, mental and physical abuse. If you're in a relationship that includes these factors, you need to get out, and get out fast. A lot people try to cover it up, and act like shit is all good but it is really not, and by covering it up it won't get any better. If you have a lot of fight in the relationship the aggressor should seek anger management or leave.

Now don't think I'm taking sides -- both parties are to blame. If you are provoking your partners then you are the cause for them lashing out, by dragging out the argument, applying verbal pressure on your partner, nagging and all the other shit to get someone mad. Think about it, if you walk away who does your partner have to argue with? For example, is your partner one of those partners who says, "oh so you don't wanna answer me" and they demand an answer, then get the fuck out of there, cause nine times out of ten it will turn violent and someone could end up hurt or worse DEAD.

Now some of you are like, Flip, why are you not being more specific and blaming the men? Well, I would have until I saw an episode of *Tyra* where women bust their men's ass. So I will say partner. I feel the person who is being assaulted shouldn't suffocate themselves by remaining in a hostile environment, and I use the word suffocate in a strong manner, because if you remain there you might as well put a bag over your head.

OK, it's like when you're young and you have a very strict parent, one who drops you off every morning, picks you up, searches your room; you can't even shit in peace. How do you think you will feel? Exactly! So the person in that relationship will feel suffocated because of the abuse and will feel like there is nowhere to run.

In my opinion, if you're the abuser seek help, because if you don't then it will be too late and you'll either be in jail, regretting what you did, or six feet under because the person got tired. I know it's not easy to walk away but try your best.

I think a man that hits a woman is a coward but not a coward because he hit her, a coward cause he wasn't brave enough to walk away. I've had fights with females, and I don't know about you guys who are reading this but that shit haunts me, and the incident replays and replays in my mind constantly. Now if you ask me why, I wouldn't know for sure but I guess it is because my parents raised me with a conscience. Now I'm a bird because why do something that I'll regret; if you going to regret it don't do it, right? Simple... right?

Now if you're being abused and the person doesn't want to stop, then get help; get out of there, love is strong but it's not stronger than the will to live. Living is a wonderful thing so don't cut your life short for what you think is love.

ACKNOWLEDGMENTS

I would like to thank the man above, the All Mighty
GOD

All my supporters cause without you who would Flip
be?

My Pride and Joy, Tessanne Marie Robinson, My
baby Girl and my son – Pierre Nicholas Robinson
aka Nekko

Lizanne Roinson, My Heart, Jaheim Cooper,
Boobie a.k.a. Lil Flip.

My Parents, (Mom) Marie Delus for always
being there and putting up with my bullshit
and helping me with my career.

Trevor Robinson, Sr. (Dad) for always encouraging
me to do well and having faith in me; if it wasn't for
him I wouldn't be the man I am today.

My Brother, Theodore Robinson, for making me
proud of him, and keepin it real.

My uncle Money Mil a.k.a. Clint Milfort, always
saying I can do better and making me understand the
business side of this game.

The HEAD of our Family my Grandmother Marie
Suzie Jean-Pierre – I Love you and thank you for
always being there for me.

Carmel Christian School, Ms Moore, Ms Macintosh,
Keith Byer, thank you all for guiding me and blessing
me with the knowledge I have today, if it wasn't for

your school and your form of teaching, I don't know where I would have ended up.

Auntie Debra and Uncle Rob for always seeing the positive side and telling me I will be all right, it's just a phase. I remember the broom (lol).

Auntie Annette for always taking care of me and anything I need; no matter what. Also my cousin Tristan "I got you".

Auntie Sheila and Uncle Pierre-paul for always having a room for me when I needed it. Also Rebecca, Marissa and Vanessa for your love.

Uncle Rodney, Auntie Sarah, Isabella, Shennia, Jabari and Isaiah.

My Godmother, Pascal Marie Poulard, Nen Nen, for always having her doors opened for me when I need somewhere to go.

My 2nd Mom, Annie, who took care of me and my brother while my Mom serve in the Marine Corp during Desert Storm. My sis and bros Tiffany, Paul and Ananias

Auntie Karen and Uncle Joe, Lil Joe, Mike and Danny for making me part of your family.

Grandma Petroline, Uncle Tommy, Auntie Erica, Aunt Izema, Cousin Marlon, Uncle Dave – All the Whyte and Robinson

LLona, Sandra, Michelle and Patrick for your friendship and support helped my family in many ways. A special thanks to Sandra for all you thought me about girls and protections.

Auntie Elaine, Samantha, Quanna, Wenter, Auntie Shell, Rip Auntie Liz. They helped mold me into the man I am today.

Black House Pooh for recording my 1st record and being there throughout my career and for helping me get on the radio.

Skem Henry Kapreli, Big Wing Production, for spending lots of money on me, and helping me in my career, we made a lot of songs together and he made me want to take music more serious.

Dj G Money for spinning my records and really breaking me as an artist to the tri-state.

Scenario, The World's Greatest Film Director, for shooting all my videos and making my imagery great for the World to see.

Team Lite Werk, for being my bros for life, Hitz, Pretty P, Kz, Gt Nuk, Money mix.

Bynoe for being a great friend and having faith in me.

Stack Bundles for guiding me and taking me on the road with him when I was a nobody and for being a great Mentor. RIP

My Cousin Nicholas Whyte for accepting me and letting me appreciate the smaller things in life, and always having my back, a person who I look up to and forever will. RIP

My Cousin (P Dot), Pierre Paul Jean Paul, for being my road dog for life, and backing me up anywhere, anytime, and making me realize that being yourself is the best way to live, regardless of the haters. RIP

Benny the Jeweler, for supporting me through my whole career and having faith in me and providing me with the best jewelry in the world.

Step It Up Auto Sound for looking out and hooking up all my cars.

Shout outs, Tanean my best friend; Eazy, my bro for life; if I need him he there; Kyah Baby my sister; Joe Money; Caspa; Bri Beauty; 1st Lady of The Retro Kidz ;Angie; Young B; my right hand Lou; Merrick 118 The Block; Taylor Mayde; Young Celeb; Dj Webstar; Jim Jones; Web n Nitty; my cousin Joka (Tone, four Mstars), we been thru it all; Ms Vogelzon for taking me in; Snow; Moet Girls; Christina my favorite person from L.I.; Janea; and the rest of you guys a.k.a., Laundrymat On Wheels (Meaning you guys make house calls to wash people up).

And The Whole Queens NY Stand Up

Oh yea, Nailah Reid, you been my friend for the longest, and you're my first love. I really appreciate the impact you have on my life, even tho we fuss and fight.   Ms Reid; I didn't forgot u

Aunti Erica, Ebony and Amber

The Mcfadden family: Ms Mcfadden, Mr Mcfadden, Ivroy, Talia, Candice a.k.a. kd, Julius, d

kno money, and RIP Tone Macc, man it hurts me they took ya life, bro, but ima hold you down with the fam

RIP Gbaby miss u baiiiii

RIP Ricky love u

E and Tear from Hall of Fame, for helping me spread my music

out to Mervin perch. For always keeping it real, and Sylviana Gunness, for supporting me also

Lou for being my best friend, and holding me down for all these years

Lou's mom (Annette Toe)

The whole FYL, LBG, TPO, 111 Ave., the whole 40 projects, Baisley, Cambria Heights

And Rockaway, Blvd., my boy Rumbles and Payback I got back for life

The entire Fiscal Ops (my Mom job) supporters during our struggles such as: Kiesha, Carmen, Sharise, Adrienne, Maritza, Bob R., Alan R., Ella and all the past and current staff members. RIP Jim Atkinson

Max for your help

Everyone else who support and had a direct impact on my life; sorry if I didn't mention you by name but know I remember and appreciate you.